W9-CAO-562

McCall Collection of Modern Art

MODERN FRENCH MASTERS
The Impressionists

Published by Fratelli Fabbri Editori
Publishers, Milan, Italy, and
The McCall Publishing Company,
New York, New York

PUBLISHED IN ITALY UNDER THE TITLE
Mensile D' Arte

Library of Congress Catalog Card Number 79-105945
SBN8415-1000-8

IMPRESSIONISM

In the second half of the nineteenth century a new art movement was born in France. It was derisively christened "Impressionism" by a French art critic upon seeing a painting by Claude Monet called *Impression — Sunrise* at a group showing of young artists in 1874. Actually the derisive name was an accurate one, and it soon lost its mocking connotation, for "impressions" were precisely what these artists were trying to convey in their paintings.

New interest in light

The chief concern of Impressionist painters was light. They felt that no artist in all the history of European painting had ever really succeeded in painting light. And so they took their easels out of doors, into the fresh air and sunshine, and painted what they saw. They were no longer interested in painting landscapes in their studios, as artists had done before them. They were no longer interested in historical and mythological subjects taken from classical antiquity, but painted the things that they saw around them.

Although their compositions and colors were carefully planned, their paintings seemed casual and spontaneous in comparison to the contrived and artificial manner of the Academicians.

New painting technique

And they invented a new "vocabulary" of paint and a new technique for applying it, in order to express their new, visual approach to nature and society. They used purer, lighter colors, and often, instead of mixing the paint on their palettes, applied strokes of pure color directly to the canvas and let the eye of the beholder blend them. These strokes might be various shades of one color applied side by side, for intensity and luminosity, or they might be many different colors, for the Impressionists, in their attempt to depict light, broke up their colors rather in the way a prism breaks up a ray of sunlight. Even shadows glowed with many colors in tiny strokes of paint—red, yellow, blue, green.

New type of subject

In their enthusiasm over their new discoveries these artists tirelessly recorded the multiple aspects of nature and of contemporary life. They painted the seacoast with its brilliant light and changing cloud forms, quiet village streets, picnics in the open air, regattas and horse races, the animation of passers-by on Parisian boulevards, the intent play of children in leafy parks, the gaiety of dance halls and cafes and theaters. Practically every facet of French life was caught on canvas with a felicity of expression that was just short of miraculous. No writer has given us as true and complete a picture of the period as did the Impressionists, who are the real historians and poets of their time, of its society and customs and daily life.

The Impressionists were a remarkably intimate and homogeneous group of friends. They worked together, ate and drank together, exhibited together, learned from each other, and helped each other in time of trouble. The group included Monet, Renoir, Pissarro, Sisley, Bazille, Morisot and Cassatt. Manet and Degas must be considered with the group too, as they were so intimately involved with it, but they were not really Impressionists.

For the sake of convenience—and only for the sake of convenience, as obviously no artistic movement can be said to have any precise beginning or end—we might take 1863 as the beginning of Impressionism. That was the year of the famous "Show of Rejected Artists," the Salon des Refusés.

The Salon des Refusés

The jury of the annual "official" art show at the all-powerful Salon had been particularly severe that year. The number of would-be artists had increased so alarmingly, they said, that it was necessary to build a dam in front of them. Such a great number of paintings had been rejected—more than four thousand—that the Emperor Napoleon III, responding to the furious outcry of artists and the press, ordered an exhibition of the rejects.

It was the first time in history that a group of progressive artists had been given the opportunity to protest against official art. Until then the Salon had ruled the world of French art with despotic and unchallenged power. It was one of the few places where an artist could exhibit his work. There were some dealers, but private art galleries as we have them today did not exist. The Salon also influenced public commissions and museum purchases as well as purchases by individuals.

So refusal by the one authority was an extremely bitter blow to an artist. And the taste of the Salon was for grandiose, neoclassic subjects, generally with some moral connotation, painted with an enamel-like finish in subdued colors.

Boudin and Jongkind

Among the artists whose works were exhibited in this show of "radicals" were two, Boudin and Jongkind, who were particularly influential in the development of the Impressionist movement because of their interest in the rendition of light and atmosphere. Boudin was a sailor's son from the coastal town of Honfleur, and he and Jongkind frequently painted there together. The area, where the Seine flows into the English Channel, has been called the birthplace of Impressionism.

At that time Boudin and Jongkind were almost alone among European artists in preferring to paint outdoors. Other artists occasionally made preliminary sketches directly from nature, but then they returned to their studios to paint the finished picture. Boudin and Jongkind believed, however—and it was a revolutionary belief at that time—that only by painting the entire canvas in the open air could they achieve the effects of immediacy, the "impressions" of shimmering light and constantly changing atmospheric conditions that they desired.

This belief Boudin instilled in the young Monet, then only seventeen years old, who wrote, after going on a painting expedition with the older artist, "It was as if a veil had suddenly been torn from my eyes. I understood. I grasped what painting could really be."

Much later, in his modest autobiography, Boudin wrote: "I may well have had some small measure of influence on the movement that led painters to study actual daylight and express the changing aspects of the sky with the utmost sincerity." But he also wrote, attesting to his debt to his friend Jongkind, "I came in by the door which he had already forced."

Whistler

The American artist Whistler also exhibited in the Salon des Refusés of 1863. He was not so much interested in effects of light as in harmonies of neutral tones and arrangements of color patterns. His work seemed more carefully planned, less casual and spontaneous and naturalistic than that of the Impressionists.

Whistler was an eccentric and egotistical dandy whose flamboyant and affected costume inspired Degas to remark, "You behave, my friend, as though you had no talent!" He was also sensitive and introspective and his paintings reflect his personality. They are subtle, polished, melancholy, concerned more with sentiment than with full-bodied emotion. Often in his painting he takes a single color and weaves it into delicate harmonies, as in his *Symphony in White No. I: The White Girl* (Plate 6) and *Nocturne in Blue and Gold: The Old Bridge at Battersea* (Plate 7).

The latter comes alive in his own lyrical lines—for he was something of a poet, too—"and when the rising mist clothes the riverside... as with a veil, and the poor buildings lose themselves in the dim sky... and the whole city hangs in the heavens... then nature, who for once has sung in tune, sings her exquisite song to the artist alone, her son and master."

Many of the rejected paintings, including Whistler's, aroused in the public and critics mere indifference or mild ridicule, but one painting inspired them to outrage. It became the scandal of the show—and in the shocked interest that it aroused it very possibly advanced the cause of modern art a great deal! The painting was *Le Déjeuner sur l'Herbe* (Plate 8) by Manet. It shows two fully clothed young men sitting on the grass with a nude young woman, while another young woman, clad only in a transparent white shift, approaches from a stream where she has evidently been bathing.

Manet

What shocked the Parisian public was not the nudity of the young woman in the painting, but the realism with which it was depicted. The public had seen many paintings of nudes, but these were idealized female forms representing Venus or Diana or a nymph or muse. This young woman was not a nymph but a Parisian model, very realistically painted. The public was offended, the critics irate, the Emperor pronounced the picture "immodest" and the Empress turned her embarrassed gaze elsewhere.

Manet had not, of course, intended that his painting should be "read" in a literal way. Inspired by a painting by Giorgione called *Concert Champêtre*, and basing his composition on a painting by Raphael, he had worked the theme into a conception entirely his own, an arrangement of forms and colors that was not intended to portray reality.

He composed another variation on a theme by Giorgione when he painted his famous (at the time it was considered infamous) canvas entitled *Olympia.* The inspiration for the picture was Giorgione's *Sleeping Venus,* and again the public was shocked to see that the nude in the painting was quite obviously not a goddess, but resembled, as Zola said, "many young women about whom everybody knows." And as if that were not enough, she stared out at the spectator so impudently and so provocatively that she seemed to be including him in her environment of wickedness.

But in this painting, as in the earlier one, the realism with which the subject is treated does not mean that it is to be interpreted literally. It is simply a motif that Manet has taken from a Renaissance master and reworked on his own terms, almost as if he were playing a kind of game with it.

Manet's technique was also offensive to the public taste; people preferred the ultra-smooth surfaces of academic paintings to his comparatively rough brushwork. And instead of modeling his forms with gradual shading from light to dark, he painted in flat areas of color that were relatively unmodeled.

Such critical opprobrium hurt Manet deeply. His friend Baudelaire scolded him for his sensitivity. "It's really stupid that you should get so worked up. You're laughed at, your merits are not appreciated. So what? Do you think you're the first man to be in that position?"

Effects of the Salon des Refusés

In spite of the scorn and abuse of the critics, in spite of the fact that the public came to the Salon des Refusés only to deride it, still it was not without significance and accomplishment. Its effects, although accidental, were important. It made a definite break between established art and the progressive rebels and set a precedent for the latter's independent show, which would come ten years later. And it brought to the public attention—even though the attention manifested itself as ridicule—the new and radical developments in the art world. It also made Manet the hero of the hour and the acknowledged leader of the young artists of the avant-garde.

In the same year, 1863, Manet had his first one-man show in Paris. One of the paintings exhibited was *Concert in the Tuileries Gardens* (Plate 10). Here his choice of subject perhaps reflects the fact that he came of a prosperous family and moved with ease and pleasure in the elegant world of fashion. His appearance and social position were in marked contrast to the public conception of him as an unwashed revolutionary. Baudelaire had said, "Give us a modern painter who can show how great and poetic we are in our frock coats and our patent leather boots." This painting may have been Manet's answer. Even a picture as apparently inoffensive as this one so enraged one of the viewers that he tried to slash it with his cane.

Paradoxically, although Manet was considered revolutionary by the public and many of the critics, to the younger painters with whom he became associated he seemed a traditionalist, a master from an older generation whom they recognized as their leader but who had some slightly dated habits to be overcome. At the time of the Salon des Refusés, Manet was still painting only in his studio. He refused to paint even landscapes out of doors.

In his controversial *Le Déjeuner sur l'Herbe* he uses flat planes of light, without any convincing source for this light, something an out-of-door painter would not have done.

But after his contact with the Impressionists, especially Monet, he underwent a change of heart. He was not too proud to learn from his young friends and became, like them, enamored of light and air and of the enchanting and ever-changing spectacle of contemporary life. His palette became lighter, his brush strokes freer, and the feeling of his paintings more spontaneous.

In the end, however, he could not completely accept his friends' beliefs. He refused to exhibit with them, and continued to feel that the Salon represented "the only real field of battle." However revolutionary his paintings may have seemed, he was not, himself, a revolutionary. There is an interesting contrast between his conservative character and his artistic independence.

His friends' influence on him was deep, but his own artistic personality was too strong to be subdued. He retained an Impressionistic feeling for light and color, but returned to his former carefully thought-out compositions and concern for solid forms.

The masterpiece of his last years is *A Bar at the Folies-Bergère* (Plate 48). It is a beautifully composed painting and a fascinating medley of lights and forms and textures, completely plausible in its design and completely impossible as an accurate representation of actuality. The barmaid's reflection is detached at an impossible angle, the reflection of the man upon whom she is waiting is overlarge, the reflected bottles to the left of her figure do not coincide in shape or position with the bottles on the marble counter.

But Manet's purpose was not to represent actuality. It was to create a brilliant, sparkling, glittering, animated impression that is, beneath its appearance of spontaneity, carefully, even meticulously, organized. His canvas is a world in itself, whose laws do not always coincide with the laws of the real world. It is a prime example of what Degas meant when he said, with his customary elegant wit, "A painting is an artificial work existing outside nature, and it requires as much knavery, trickery and deceit as the perpetration of a crime."

With this painting Manet attained, a year before his death, at least a degree of success and acclaim. But, in his own words, "It comes too late to compensate for twenty years of failure."

Degas

Degas, like his friend Manet, was born into an aristocratic and worldly environment. He was a banker's son, a traditionalist of discriminating taste and rare intelligence who contemplated the elegance of the eighteenth century with a degree of nostalgia: "They were dirty, perhaps, but distinguished. We are clean, but we are common."

At the age of twenty he gave up the study of law and entered the School of Fine Arts, and the following year he went to Italy to study the Italian painters he had learned to admire during long hours in the Louvre. While in Florence he painted his aunt, the Baroness Bellelli, and her family (Plate 11). Already he shows here his tendency for that strong but rather curious composition that may have been his most original contribution to Impressionism, and his feeling for character in the posing of the figures. The naturalness of the setting, the parlor in the Bellelli home, also heightens this feeling for character.

Shortly after his return to Paris he made the acquaintance of Manet, and a firm but turbulent friendship began. Their work had much in common, but differed principally in that Degas gave chief importance to line, while Manet expressed form through color. Both became supreme illustrators of the Paris of their time.

Degas was interested in people rather than landscape, and he had an extraordinary eye for the gesture with which a subject reveals himself. He frequently chose to paint awkwardness or inelegance, what he called "attractive ugliness," as in the pose of the seated ballerina of *The Rehearsal* (Plate 40) and *After the Bath: Woman Drying Her Feet* (Plate 60). He liked to go behind the scenes or, as he said, "to peek through the keyhole." His subjects frequently give the impression of having been caught off guard, but his elegance of style prevents their ever appearing as ugly.

Degas disagreed with the Impressionists in many ways. He rarely worked out of doors. The physical discomfort involved in outdoor painting did not appeal to his fastidious taste, and he did not share his friends' enthusiasm for painting changeable atmospheric conditions and brilliant sunshine. He had a predilection for drawing and for line, whereas they dispensed with line almost entirely. He did not care for the spontaneous effect that was their aim, but affirmed crisply, "There is nothing less spontaneous than my art." He made preliminary sketches directly from the subject, but composed his paintings in his studio with the greatest care.

Many of his subjects were chosen from the nighttime world of theaters and cafes. *Café Concert at les Ambassadeurs* (Plate 36) is an example of his careful composition disguised as spontaneity. The line of lights, creating a diagonal to the left of the singer, is continued in the line of her outstretched arm. A second diagonal is established by her other arm and shoulder and the two larger lights, and the intersection of these diagonals makes her face the primary focal point. The exaggerated enlargement of the bass fiddle necks in the foreground here and in *Rehearsal on the Stage* (Plate 41) serves to emphasize the space between foreground and background.

Much of the originality of Degas' composition is due to the influence of Japanese prints. The vantage point from which he views his subject is frequently unconventional, as is his perspective. And like the Japanese printmaker, he sometimes permits his figures to be cut off by the frame of the picture.

But line was his great delight. As an old man, nearly blind, he said to a friend, "Let there be no eulogies at my funeral. Say only, 'He loved to draw.'"

Monet, the "arch-impressionist"

The artist who has come to be considered the "Arch-Impressionist" is Monet. It was one of his paintings that gave the movement its name, and it is his work that best exemplifies its ideas.

Monet was a grocer's son from Le Havre. His early career as a caricaturist was broken off when Boudin advised him to take up a more serious kind of art. Painting outdoors at Honfleur and Le Havre with Boudin and Jongkind, he discovered that color is everywhere, even in the deepest shadows. He learned that complementary colors enhance each other: a blue-violet shadow sets off a spot of orange-yellow sunlight. He saw that two objects placed side by side give color to each other.

On one of their excursions Jongkind painted two pictures of the same subject, a cathedral, from the same position but at different times of day, one in the cold light of morning and the other in the warm, evening light. This was the seed from which, thirty years later, grew Monet's series of paintings of the façade of Rouen Cathedral in different lights (Plate 53). Pursuing the same studies of light, he painted a series of pictures of haystacks at different times of day, of the Thames in London and, very much later, the waterlilies in his pond at Giverny (Plate 58), in which he approaches abstraction.

After the Salon des Refusés of 1863 all the young Impressionists admired Manet and, inspired by his *Le Déjeuner sur l'Herbe,* Monet painted a large figure composition in the open air to which, perhaps as a tribute, he gave the same title (Plate 17). It shows a much greater unity between figures and background than the earlier picture and has a definite "outdoor" feeling in comparison with Manet's painting. But the use of flat areas of color and the elimination of half tones derive from Manet. Only two fragments of this painting remain, as the large canvas, left with a fellow artist as security for unpaid rent, was rolled up and allowed to molder in the course of a few years.

In 1870, at the outbreak of the Franco-Prussian War, Monet fled to England. He was a socialist and saw no reason why he should give his life for the Emperor. Upon his return to France he settled at Argenteuil, on the Seine not far from Paris. There he painted, often in the company of Renoir and Manet, in a boat fitted out as a studio (Plates 26 and 31).

He painted his first truly great Impressionist canvases there. His colors were brighter than before and he discovered that their brilliance could be increased if they are mixed by the eye rather than by the brush or palette knife. A stroke of blue applied next to a stroke of yellow, he found, can result in a much more intense green than if the pigments are mixed before being applied to the canvas.

Although this period was a high point in Monet's achievement, it was also a time of desperate poverty. It is said that Renoir stole bread from his mother's table to keep Monet's family from starving. At one time, in an agony of despair over his wife's illness and his complete lack of funds, Monet attempted suicide. But the despair engendered by his physical want never made itself apparent in his paintings. His triumphantly gay and spirited *Rue Montargueil with Flags* (Plate 37) was done at this time. "I paint as a bird sings," he said.

First Impressionist Exhibition

The idea of holding a group show was one that Monet and his friends had cherished for some time before they were able to realize it. Finally, in 1874, they pooled their resources, rented a photographer's studio and set up the first Impressionist Exhibition. Monet was the leading spirit and Degas helped enthusiastically, even though he was not an Impressionist; Manet, however, declined to join them. Thirty-nine artists exhibited, among them Monet, Degas, Renoir, Pissarro, Cézanne, Morisot and Boudin.

The ridicule inspired by the show is now legendary. Viewers found that the colors were "so raw that they hurt their eyes," and that the distortions of form were comical if not offensive. Any hope the exhibitors had entertained of selling their pictures was soon abandoned.

Undaunted, the Impressionists tried again two years later and were received with a critical tirade even worse than that which had greeted their earlier show. "A new disaster is overwhelming the district," one critic wrote. "There has just opened an exhibition of so-called painting.... Five or six lunatics—among them a woman [Berthe Morisot]—have met there to exhibit their works....Try to make Monsieur Pissarro understand that trees are not violet and that sky is not the color of fresh butter. Try to explain to Monsieur Renoir that a woman's torso is not a mass of flesh in the process of decomposition, with green and purple patches like a corpse in a state of utter putrefaction....Yesterday a poor soul was arrested who, after having seen the exhibition, was biting the passers-by."

Renoir

In spite of what critical diatribe might lead one to believe, Renoir was one of the earliest of the Impressionists to be accepted by the public, perhaps because warmth and pleasure are such obvious qualities of his work. In his student days his master said to him, "One doesn't paint for amusement, Monsieur Renoir," and Renoir retorted, "If it didn't amuse me, believe me, I wouldn't paint!" His pictures show very plainly the pleasure he experienced in painting them as well as the gusto with which he enjoyed the life they represent, and this double pleasure is communicated to the viewer.

Early in their careers Renoir and Monet often painted together, in styles that are barely distinguishable (Plates 18 and 19). Then his own style asserted itself. The influence of his early apprenticeship to a porcelain painter is apparent in the delicate and precise touch of his brush and in his love of the fragile, graceful, sensuous charm of the eighteenth century, which he translated into terms of his own time. His emotional warmth and robust love of the physical world show in his handling of colors and textures—the pearlescent smoothness of a woman's skin, the translucence of a silken sleeve, the crisp-soft petals of chrysanthemums. In group compositions light, especially dappled sunlight, is characteristically used to unite his figures with each other and with their surroundings (Plates 29 and 32).

It has been said of Renoir that he had the reaction to life of "an adolescent who glories in luscious food and plump, pink girls." Certainly he was not an intellectual. He deplored his friends' habit of sitting for half the night in a cafe, theorizing about art. "Don't ask me whether painting ought to be subjective or objective. I don't give a damn!" His friends would do better, he said, to get to bed at a decent hour so that they could get up to paint in the morning. But if he was less subtle as a person than Manet and Degas, he was also more likable. His social ease and pleasant manner did much to erase the public conception of the Impressionist as a wild-eyed, slightly mad Bohemian anarchist.

In his later years Renoir's style changed. "I had wrung Impressionism dry," he said. "It was a blind alley as far as I was concerned." His work was influenced by a trip to Italy, where he was particularly impressed by the paintings of Raphael and by the frescoes at Pompeii. He continued to paint with all the sensuous color and love of life that he had showed earlier, but his work achieved a solidity and monumentality that were new.

Pissarro

The oldest of the Impressionists and the one who, next to Monet, most consistently followed its doctrines was Pissarro. He was also the most influential in that he was guide and teacher to Cézanne, Van Gogh and Gauguin; their debt to him is enormous. He was a generous, steadfast, sober man, the patriarch of the movement, to whom Zola wrote: "You must realize that you won't please anyone. . . .Then why the devil do you have the errant effrontery to paint solidly and to study nature frankly?. . .You are a great blunderer, Sir: you are a painter whom I like."

This "humble and colossal" man, as Cézanne called him, was by political conviction a socialist-anarchist, and an avowed atheist, but there was no hate in him. He was a quiet and gentle man who was held in the highest esteem by all his friends. He was a gifted teacher who had a deep respect for the opinions and personality of others. In a letter to his artist sons he said, "What I fear most is for you to resemble me too much. Accept only those of my opinions that are in accord with your sentiments and mode of understanding. Be bold, then, and to work!"

Unlike his Impressionist friends he was accepted by the official Salon more often than not. Between 1860 and 1870 his work was shown in seven exhibits out of ten. But out of loyalty to his friends he decided to cut himself off from the Salon and show his paintings only with the Impressionist group. He was the only artist who exhibited at all eight of the Impressionist shows as well as the Salon des Refusés of 1863.

The Franco-Prussian War brought financial ruin to Pissarro's father and threw Pissarro completely on his own resources as a painter. In the German invasion of 1870 his home was occupied and almost all of his paintings, the work of fifteen years, were stolen or destroyed. He fled to England, like Monet, and worked there for the duration of the war.

After the war he returned to France, to Pontoise. There he was joined by Cézanne, who said of him, "He was the one among the painters who came closest to nature." Whatever Pissarro painted, however simple his subject, a rutted road or a field of cabbages, he infused it with poetry. He painted in all weather and in all seasons. A sketch by an artist friend shows him as an old man standing before his easel in a field, a large, battered felt hat on his head, his easel hung with weights to hold it against the wind.

He is sometimes accused of dullness because poverty forced him to paint even when inspiration failed, but his art should not, for that reason, be underrated. The best of his works have a luminous quality that is unsurpassed by any of the other Impressionists.

Sisley

The work of Sisley, except for less delicate brushwork, strongly resembles that of Pissarro. But, unlike Pissarro, Sisley never painted figures. He was a landscapist exclusively. He had a natural feeling for landscape, preferably with water. He painted the river Loing when he lived in the village of Moret and the Seine when he lived at Marly. In England he painted the Thames and the Severn.

Sisley's father was a fairly affluent English businessman, and until 1871 Sisley did not paint for a living, but simply as an amateur with a passionate desire to paint. After the war, however, he was forced to support himself by his art, and his struggle for recognition was a pathetic one. He was a proud and dedicated artist who was forced to beg for buyers.

There are a number of letters on record in which he asks his friends to buy his paintings for very modest sums. He felt confident that recognition would soon come to him and the paintings would increase in value to the point where his friends would realize a considerable profit. All he wanted was peace of mind so that he could continue to work.

In their time of want, both Sisley and Renoir were befriended by a kindly pastry cook named Murer, who was a great lover of art. They would eat in the little restaurant at the back of Murer's shop, and when their dinner tabs added up to fifty francs or so, Murer would be pleased to accept a painting in exchange and would hang it on the wall of the shop. Eventually the profits from the shop permitted him to retire and take up painting himself. "In this cursed trade," he said, "if pastry is only a week old it must be sold cheap. You are cleverer than that, you artists. You deal in goods that keep indefinitely, and even improve with keeping."

There are few more poignant proofs of the truth that an artist is appreciated only after his death than the records of Paris auctions of Sisley's work. In 1865, at an auction of Impressionist canvases, his pictures brought an average of 100 francs apiece (about $5.00). Three months after his death they sold for forty times as much, 4,100 francs apiece (about $200). And a year later one of the three painting he did of the flood at Marly, which are considered his masterpieces (Plate 38), brought at auction 43,000 francs (about $2,000).

Bazille

There were a number of other artists in the Impressionist group who were able and accomplished as artists, but who were not great forces in the movement. One of these was Bazille. With Monet, Sisley, and Renoir, he was one of the original quartet of young future Impressionists studying at Gleyre's studio. He was killed in the Franco-Prussian War before either he or the movement had had time to develop significantly.

Caillebotte

Caillebotte was an amateur painter of professional stature and one of the very first collectors of Impressionist work. He willed his collection of sixty-five paintings by Manet, Degas, Pissarro, Sisley, Renoir, Monet, and Cézanne to the French government, which was embarrassed by the bequest and in the end accepted only three-fifths of it.

Morisot

Two women painters of great talent were members of the Impressionist group, both from wealthy and cultivated families. Berthe Morisot was a good friend as well as sister-in-law of Manet, and posed for him many times (Plate 24). Her paintings are usually feminine in subject, but done in a style so vigorous and sure that it seems almost masculine. She believed that true realism was impossible, that every artist of necessity puts something of himself into his subject.

A friend said of her: "The interesting thing about Berthe Morisot was that she lived her paintings and painted her life. As a girl, wife and mother her sketches and paintings follow her own existence closely.... Her work reminds one of a woman's diary written in color and line."

Berthe Morisot was herself aware of this. Her painting was her conscious struggle against the pitiless obliteration of time. "I have often thought," she said, "that immortality could be the trace that our lives might leave behind."

Cassatt

As Morisot was the friend of Manet and admirer of his work, so Mary Cassatt was the friend and admirer of Degas. A young American from Philadelphia, of firm conviction and independent mind, and determined to be an artist, she arrived in Paris in 1874 after six years of independent study in the museums of Italy, Spain and Holland.

Although her study had been along traditional lines, she refused to align herself with the Academicians and was immediately drawn to the Impressionists. In the window of a picture dealer she saw a pastel drawing by Degas and knew instantly that it was the kind of art that she wanted to create herself. At almost the same time Degas became aware of her when he saw one of her paintings in the Salon of that year and remarked, "Here is one who feels as I do."

They did not meet, however, for almost three years. In 1877 Degas was introduced to her and invited her to join the Impressionist group. She accepted with delight. "I hated conventional art. Now I began to live," she said.

Her life was her art, and little else. She painted in her studio from eight in the morning until dark, and in the evening occupied herself with her graphic work in various techniques. Her subjects were women and children, and she treated them not in a sentimental way but only with great tenderness. Her interest in line equaled that of Degas. "We have identical intellectual dispositions," he said, "and an identical predilection for drawing."

Influence of Impressionism

What were Impressionism's greatest contributions to art? Perhaps most important is the emancipation of the artist from dull, dark colors to pure, bright ones as a result of his effort to portray natural light. Important, too, is a new economy of design in comparison to many earlier pictures that were cluttered with too much detail. Manet said, "Conciseness in art is a necessity and an elegance. The verbose painter bores. Who will get rid of all these trimmings?" Impressionism sought to answer that question by eliminating, in the swiftness of the recorded impression, all unnecessary detail. And a third contribution is the new attitude of the Impressionist painter to his subject. The painting was more important to him than what he painted. Bazille said, "In my opinion the subject matters little provided that what I do is interesting as a painting. I have chosen to paint our own age because that is what I understand best, because it is alive, and because I am painting for living people."

PLATES

The Forerunners of Impressionism

PLATE 1 JOHAN BARTHOLD JONGKIND *Harbor at Evening* (43.5 x 62 cm) Otterlo, Rijksmuseum Kröller-Müller

PLATE 2 EUGENE BOUDIN *Bathers on the Beach at Trouville*, 1869 (31 x 48 cm) Paris, Louvre

PLATE 3 EUGENE BOUDIN *Trouville*, 1864 (37 x 58.5 cm) Lyons, Musée des Beaux-Arts

PLATE 4 HENRI FANTIN-LATOUR *"The Engagement" Still Life*, 1869 (32 x 29 cm) Grenoble, Musée des Beaux-Arts

PLATE 5 HENRI FANTIN-LATOUR *Narcissus and Tulips*, 1862 (44 x 37 cm) Paris, Louvre

Whistler 1862

PLATE 7 JAMES MCNEILL WHISTLER *Nocturne in Blue and Gold: The Old Bridge at Battersea*, c. 1872-75, (67 x 51) London, Tate Gallery

PLATE 6 JAMES MCNEILL WHISTLER *Symphony in White No. I: The White Girl*, 1862 (216 x 109 cm) Washington, D.C., National Gallery of Art, Harris Whittemore Collection

The Golden Age of Impressionism

PLATE 8 EDOUARD MANET *The Picnic (Le Déjeuner sur l'Herbe),* 1862-63 (214 x 270 cm) Paris, Louvre

PLATE 9 EDGAR DEGAS *The Duke and Duchess Morbilli* (132 x 91 cm) Boston, Museum of Fine Arts (Gift of R. Treat Paine)

PLATE 10 EDOUARD MANET *Concert in the Tuileries Gardens*, 1862 (72 x 119 cm) London, National Gallery

PLATE 11 EDGAR DEGAS *The Bellelli Family*, 1859-60 (200 x 253 cm) Paris, Louvre

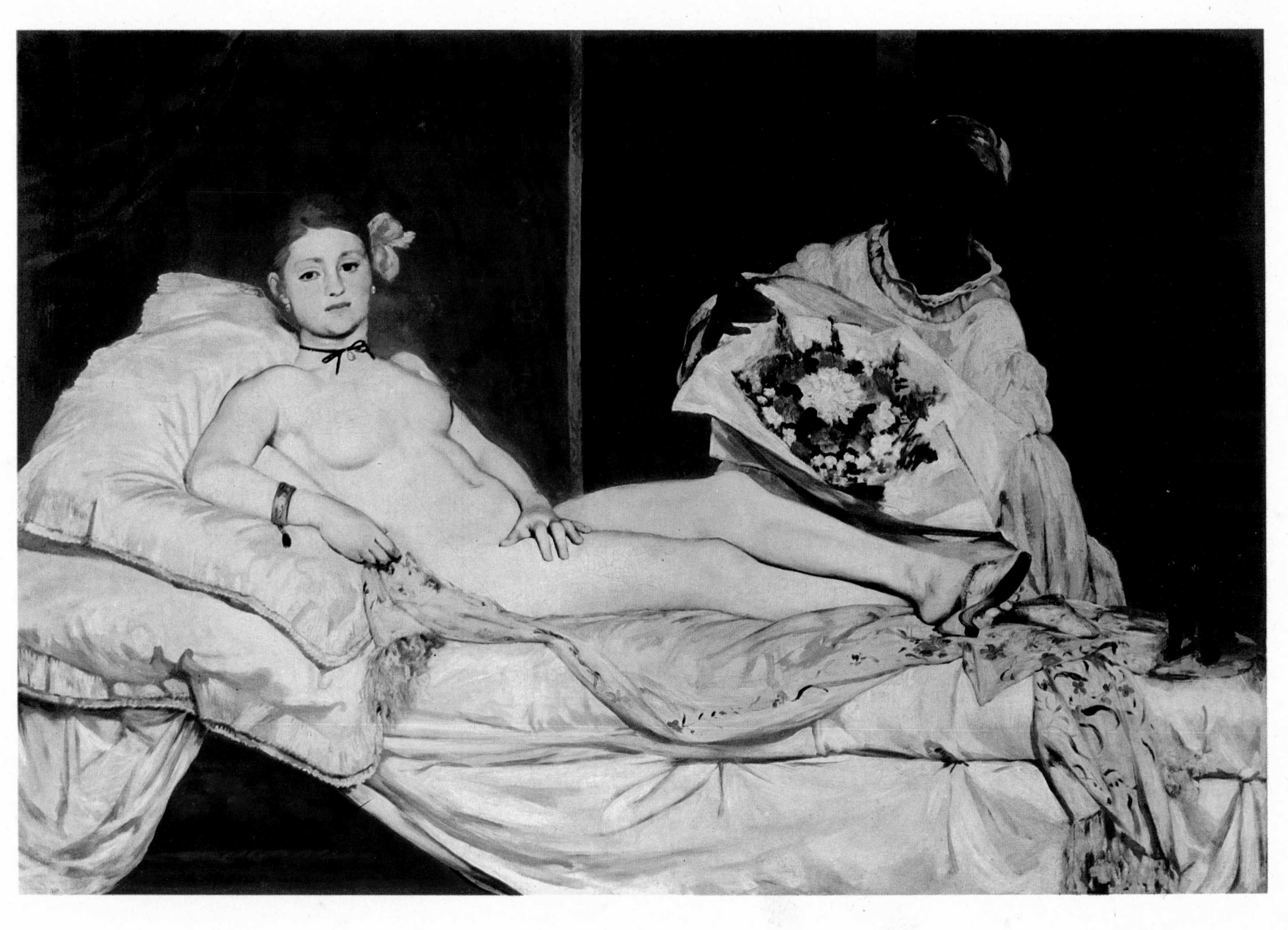

PLATE 12 EDOUARD MANET *Olympia*, 1863 (130 x 190 cm) Paris, Louvre

PLATE 13 EDGAR DEGAS *Portrait of Hortense Valpinçon,* 1869 (91 x 117 cm) Minneapolis, Institute of Arts

PLATE 14 EDOUARD MANET *Execution of the Emperor Maximilian*, 1867 (252 x 305 cm) Mannheim, Städtische Kunsthalle

PLATE 15 EDOUARD MANET *Portrait of Emile Zola,* 1868 (190 x 111 cm) Paris, Louvre

The Grand Era of Impressionism

PLATE 16 CLAUDE MONET *Terrace at Sainte-Adresse*, 1866 (96 x 127 cm) New York, Metropolitan Museum of Art

PLATE 17 CLAUDE MONET *The Picnic (Le Déjeuner sur l'Herbe)* (detail) 1865 (418 x 150 cm) Paris, Louvre

PLATE 18 CLAUDE MONET *La Grenouillère,* 1869 (73 x 99 cm) New York, Metropolitan Museum of Art, Havemeyer Collection

PLATE 19 PIERRE AUGUSTE RENOIR *La Grenouillère*, 1869 (66 x 79 cm) Stockholm, National Museum

PLATE 20 ALFRED SISLEY *The Saint-Martin Canal,* 1870 (50 x 65 cm) Paris, Louvre

PLATE 21 CAMILLE PISSARRO *Entrance to the Village of Voisins,* 1872 (45 x 55 cm) Paris, Louvre

PLATE 22 ALFRED SISLEY *Snow at Louveciennes*, c. 1874 (47 x 56 cm) London, Courtauld Institute

PLATE 23 CAMILLE PISSARRO *Pontoise, The Road to Gisors in Winter,* 1873 (60 x 79 cm) Boston, Museum of Fine Arts

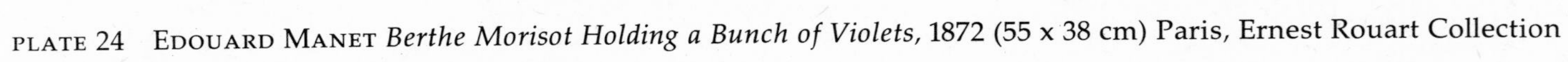
PLATE 24 EDOUARD MANET *Berthe Morisot Holding a Bunch of Violets*, 1872 (55 x 38 cm) Paris, Ernest Rouart Collection

PLATE 25 EDOUARD MANET *On the Beach,* 1873 (57 x 72 cm) Paris, Louvre

PLATE 26 EDOUARD MANET *Claude Monet Working on His Boat in Argenteuil*, 1874 (80 x 98 cm) Munich, Neue Pinakothek

PLATE 27 EDGAR DEGAS *At the Races*, c. 1877-80 (66 x 82 cm) Paris, Louvre

PLATE 28 PIERRE AUGUSTE RENOIR *Madame Monet Reading "Le Figaro,"* 1874 (53 x 71 cm)
Lisbon, Gulbenkian Foundation (Photo: Giraudon, Paris)

PLATE 29 PIERRE AUGUSTE RENOIR *The Swing,* 1876 (92 x 73 cm) Paris, Louvre

PLATE 30 CLAUDE MONET *Regatta at Argenteuil*, 1874 (60 x 100 cm) Paris, Louvre

PLATE 31 CLAUDE MONET *The Studio-Boat*, c. 1874 (50 x 64 cm) Otterlo, Rijksmuseum Kröller-Müller

PLATE 32 PIERRE AUGUSTE RENOIR *Le Moulin de la Galette* (detail), 1876 (131 x 175 cm) Paris, Louvre

PLATE 33 PIERRE AUGUSTE RENOIR *The First Outing (La Première Sortie)*, 1876 (65 x 50 cm) London, Tate Gallery

PLATE 34 PIERRE AUGUSTE RENOIR *The Loge*, 1874 (80 x 63.5 cm) London, Courtauld Institute

PLATE 35 PIERRE AUGUSTE RENOIR *Portrait of Madame Henriot*, 1874 (70 x 55 cm) Washington, D.C., National Gallery of Art (Gift of Adele R. Levy Fund Inc.)

PLATE 36 EDGAR DEGAS *Café Concert at les Ambassadeurs* (detail) 1876-77 (37 x 27 cm) Lyons, Musée des Beaux-Arts

PLATE 37 CLAUDE MONET *Rue Montargueil with Flags,* 1878 (62 x 33 cm) Rouen, Musée des Beaux-Arts

PLATE 38 ALFRED SISLEY *Flood at Pont-Marly*, 1876 (60 x 81 cm) Paris, Louvre

PLATE 39 CAMILLE PISSARRO *The Hermitage at Pontoise,* 1878 (54 x 65 cm) Basel, Kunstmuseum

PLATE 40 EDGAR DEGAS *The Rehearsal*, 1877 (68 x 103 cm) Glasgow, Glasgow Art Gallery and Museum, Sir William Burrell Collection

PLATE 41 EDGAR DEGAS *Rehearsal on the Stage*, 1878-79 (53 x 72 cm) New York; Metropolitan Museum of Art, Havemeyer Collection

Surrounding the Protagonists

PLATE 42 BERTHE MORISOT *Young Woman Sewing in a Garden,* 1881, Pau, Musée des Beaux-Arts

PLATE 43 BERTHE MORISOT *The Little Girl from Nice*, c. 1888-89 (64 x 52 cm) Lyons, Musée des Beaux-Arts

PLATE 44 MARY CASSATT *The Sisters*, c. 1885, Glasgow, Glasgow Art Gallery and Museum, Sir William Burrell Collection

PLATE 45 BERTHE MORISOT *The Butterfly Chase*, 1874 (46 x 56 cm) Paris, Louvre

PLATE 46 GUSTAVE CAILLEBOTTE *Paris in the Snow*, 1886, Geneva, Modern Art Fund

PLATE 47 J. B. ARMAND GUILLAUMIN *Outskirts of Paris*, 1873, Montpellier, Musée des Beaux-Arts

Impressionists after 1880

PLATE 48 EDOUARD MANET *A Bar at the Folies-Bergère*, 1881-82 (96 x 130 cm) London, Courtauld Institute

PLATE 49 EDOUARD MANET *The Model for the Folies-Bergère Bar* (detail) 1881 (54 x 34 cm) Dijon, Musée des Beaux-Arts

PLATE 50 ALFRED SISLEY *The Tugboat*, c. 1883 (55 x 73 cm) Paris, Musée du Petit Palais

PLATE 51 CAMILLE PISSARRO *The Wheelbarrow*, c. 1881 (46 x 55 cm) Paris, Louvre

PLATE 52 CLAUDE MONET *Poplars on the River Epte,* 1890 (89 x 72 cm) London, Tate Gallery

PLATE 53 CLAUDE MONET *Rouen Cathedral: The Façade in Sunlight,* 1894 (107 x 73 cm) Paris, Louvre

PLATE 54 PIERRE AUGUSTE RENOIR *Vase of Chrysanthemums* (82 x 66 cm) Rouen, Musée des Beaux-Arts

PLATE 55 Pierre Auguste Renoir *Blond Bather*, 1881 (80 x 63 cm) Turin, Private Collection

PLATE 56 ALFRED SISLEY *The Banks of the Seine: Wind Blowing*, 1894 (81 x 100 cm) Rouen, Musée des Beaux-Arts

PLATE 57 CAMILLE PISSARRO *The First February Rays at Bazincourt*, 1893 (65 x 81 cm) Otterlo, Rijksmuseum Kröller-Müller

PLATE 58 CLAUDE MONET *Waterlilies* (detail) c. 1910 (200 x 600 cm) Zurich, Kunsthaus

PLATE 59 CAMILLE PISSARRO *The Louvre, Morning, Snow Effect*, 1902 (65 x 81 cm) London, Tate Gallery

PLATE 60 EDGAR DEGAS *After the Bath: Woman Drying Her Feet*, c. 1886 (68 x 62 cm) Paris, Louvre

THE ARTISTS

JEAN FREDERIC BAZILLE

Born 1841 in Montpellier. In 1862 went to Paris to study medicine and painting, and enrolled at Gleyre's studio. There he became acquainted with Sisley, Renoir, and Monet, with whom he painted at Honfleur in 1864 and in the forest of Fontainebleau and with whom he several times shared his studio.

From 1866 to 1870 his works were almost always accepted at the Salon. Of a well-to-do family, he generously came to the aid of his friends, especially Monet. In 1870, when his work appeared rich with promise, the Franco-Prussian War broke out and he enrolled in a Zoave regiment and fell in the battle of Beaune-la-Rolande.

BAZILLE *Self-Portrait*, Paris, Louvre (Cabinet des dessins)

EUGENE BOUDIN

Born at Honfleur, near Le Havre, in 1824. Worked at first in a stationery shop but in 1845, encouraged by Millet, he devoted himself entirely to painting. In 1850 obtained a grant for three years' study in Paris. On his return to Le Havre he guided and influenced the young Monet ("If I have become a painter," said Monet, "I owe it to Eugene Boudin"), and taught him to paint out of doors, directly from his subject, studying nature "in all its variety, all its freshness."

In 1859 he met Courbet, who had a decided influence on him, helping him to overcome his shyness, and in 1862 he made the acquaintance of Jongkind, and painted with him and Monet at Le Havre. He took part in the first Impressionist show in 1874. Later he attained a certain degree of success: in 1889 he received a gold medal at the Paris World's Fair, and in 1892 was awarded the medal of the Legion of Honor.

The beach animated with groups of people, the sea and sky were his favorite subjects. He traveled in Brittany, Belgium, Holland, and Italy. Died at Deauville in 1898.

BOUDIN *Crinolines on the Beach* (1869) Paris, Private Collection

GUSTAVE CAILLEBOTTE

Born in Paris in 1848. Studied with Bonnat at the School of Fine Arts, then, discouraged, retired to Argenteuil to live and was employed as a boat builder. Here in 1874 he met Monet. Joined the Impressionist group and became very helpful to them, buying their works and aiding in the organization of their exhibitions. Took part in almost all their group shows.

A wealthy bachelor, loyal and generous, possessing as early as 1876 a notable collection of his friends' paintings, he made a will leaving his collection to the state provided it would be placed in the Louvre. At his death in 1894, however, the conditions of his will were followed only in part because of the indignation of politicians, critics, and academicians at the idea of Impressionist works in a museum.

MARY CASSATT

Daughter of a rich banker, she was born in Pittsburgh in 1845. In 1868 she went to Europe and traveled in France, Italy, Spain, and Holland, studying the works of the old masters, especially Rubens, Velasquez, and Correggio. In 1877 she met Degas, who had already seen her works in the Salon of 1874. Invited by him to join the Impressionist group and to exhibit with them, she accepted gladly. From then on she exhibited frequently with the group.

She was especially influenced by Degas, with whom she shared a feeling for drawing. Children, motherhood, scenes of family life are the recurring subjects of her pictures. She helped to spread knowledge of the Impressionists in America, influencing her family and friends to buy their works.

CASSATT *The Tramway* (1891) Paris, Bibliothèque nationale (Cabinet des étampes)

In her last years an eye disease made her almost blind. She died in 1926 at her chateau, Mesnil-Beaufresne.

EDGAR HILAIRE DEGAS

Born in Paris, July 19, 1834, son of a wealthy banker, Auguste de Gas. Finished his studies at the lyceum, and after a brief period of study with the painter Barrias he enrolled in the course of Henri Lamothe, a disciple of Ingres. But after about a year he moved to the School of Fine Arts.

In 1854 he visited Naples. He returned to Italy in 1856, stopping in Florence at the home of his uncle, Baron Bellelli. In 1858 he visited Rome, Viterbo, Orvieto (where he admired and copied Signorelli's frescoes), Perugia, Assisi and Florence, where he was again the guest of his uncle and began the painting *The Bellelli Family*. From 1860 to 1868, under the influence of Ingres and the Italian masters, he painted historical and mythological subjects. Around 1865, following his meeting with Manet and the group of artists who frequented the Café Guerbois, his interests changed and he turned gradually to subjects from contemporary life. In 1872 he began to frequent the world of the opera, introduced there by a member of the orchestra, Désiré Dihau.

After a trip to America, where he visited New Orleans, he exhibited ten works at the first Impressionist show in 1874.

In 1881 he did his first work in sculpture, modeling in wax. The following years were marked by intense activity, although his sight began to weaken. In 1886, at the eighth and final exhibit ot the Impressionist group, he showed a series of ten nudes in pastel. He made several more visits to Italy, Spain, and Morocco, then retired into al-

DEGAS *Self-Portrait* (1857) Paris, Private Collection

FANTIN-LATOUR *Homage to Delacroix* (detail) Paris, Louvre (seated, left to right: Fantin-Latour, Champleury, Baudelaire; standing, left to right: Alphonse Legros, Whistler, Manet, Bracquemond, A. de Balle)

most complete isolation. He died in Paris, September 27, 1917.

HENRI FANTIN-LATOUR

Born at Grenoble, 1836. His father was his first teacher, then Lecoq di Boisbaudran. In 1855 he was deeply impressed, as was Whistler, by the Realist Show of Courbet. He made a great many copies of works in the Louvre, where in 1857 he met Manet and a few years later Berthe Morisot. Several of Fantin-Latour's and Whistler's works, rejected by the Salon of 1859, were exhibited in the studio of the painter Bonvin, where they were seen and appreciated by Courbet, among others. In 1863 he took part in the Salon des Refusés and became acquainted with Renoir, with whom he worked at the Louvre.

In 1863, after the death of Delacroix, of whom he had been a great admirer, he painted *Homage to Delacroix,* accepted by the Salon in 1864; in 1865 he exhibited *Homage to Truth.* In these two pictures he portrays himself and a group of friends, including Manet, Whistler, Bracquemond, and Duranty. In *A Studio in the Batignolles Quarter,* exhibited in 1870, he portrays the friends who frequented the Café Guerbois, including Manet, Renoir, Monet, Zola and Bazille.

In 1874 he declined, as did Manet, to participate in the first Impressionist exhibition. His art was always definitely distinct from that of his Impressionist friends. His splendid still lifes achieved great success in England, and then in his own country. He died in 1904.

ARMAND GUILLAUMIN

Born in Paris, 1841. A great friend of Pissarro and Cézanne, he took part in the Salon des Refusés and in the first Impressionist show of 1874.

Employed in the administration of civil engineering, he could paint only in his spare time, but still he participated in all the Impressionist shows except those of 1876 and 1879. In 1886 he exhibited in the New York show organized by Durand-Ruel and in the Independent Show with Seurat and Signac.

GUILLAUMIN *Self-Portrait* (c. 1874) Laren, V. van Gogh Collection

JONGKIND *The Port at Douarnenez* (1851) Paris, Louvre (Cabinet des dessins)

In 1891 he won 100,000 francs in a lottery and was finally able to dedicate himself entirely to painting. However, he was no longer in touch with his old friends (not even Monet and Pissarro) and his painting degenerated into chromatic researches. He died in Paris in 1927.

JOHAN-BARTHOLD JONGKIND

Landscapist and precursor, like Boudin, of Impressionism. Born 1819 in Latrop, Holland. In 1845 he became a pupil of Isabey and the next year followed him to Paris.

An alcoholic, afflicted with a persecution mania, and deeply in debt, Jongkind led a dissipated life in the French capital until 1853, when he returned to Holland.

Between 1860 and 1870 he was back in Paris. Then in 1862 he went to Le Havre, where he met Monet and Boudin and painted with them during the summer, exerting a decided influence on Monet. In 1863 he took part in the Salon des Refusés, spent the following year at Honfleur, where he painted again with Boudin and Monet.

He preferred to use watercolor in the landscapes, as it was more immediate, and thus he was more capable of catching on canvas his fleeting impressions.

Died at Côte-St.-André in 1891.

EDOUARD MANET

Born in Paris, January 29, 1832, of wealthy and cultivated parents. Studied at Rollin College, where he met Antonin Proust, who was his lifelong friend and left much affectionate and exact testimony about him. Manet enjoyed drawing, visited museums and exhibits. After a period as a sailor on a transport ship he returned to Paris and took up painting under the guidance of Thomas Couture, an artist of the Academy who was famous at that time.

In 1852 he left his master's studio and made several journeys, to Vienna, Monaco, Florence, Rome, and Venice. He made copies from Titian, Tintoretto, and Velasquez, and studied more recent artists: Goya, Daumier, Delacroix, Courbet. In 1858 he formed a friendship with Baudelaire, whose influence is apparent in *Concert in the Tuileries Gardens* and in *The Absinthe Drinker*, which were offered to the Salon of 1857 and rejected. Due to the influence of Baudelaire, he became infatuated with the exotic and with Spain; in 1861 he produced *The Guitar Player* and, the following year, the pictures of Spanish dancers and the celebrated *Lola de Valence*. In 1863 he exhibited three works at the Salon des Refusés, among them the famous *Le Déjeuner sur l'Herbe*, which created a scandal in the eyes of the public and the critics, a scandal that was repeated in the Salon of 1865 by *Olympia*. His *The Fifer* was rejected by the Salon of 1866.

MANET *Self-Portrait* (c. 1875) New York, Mr. and Mrs. John L. Loeb Collection

The younger artists held him in great esteem but, even though he was on terms of intimacy with Renoir and Monet, he was not at first attracted by Impressionism. Later, however, influenced chiefly by Monet, he accepted the idea and began to paint out of doors.

In 1879 he became seriously ill but continued to work, although with great effort. In 1881 he received an award at the Salon, and at the proposal of his friend Proust, then Minister of Fine Arts, he was decorated with the medal of the Legion of Honor.

In 1882 he painted his last works: *Spring* and *A Bar at the Folies-Bergère,* both exhibited at the Salon. He died in Paris, April 30, 1883.

CLAUDE MONET

Born in Paris, November 14, 1840. At five he moved with his family to Le Havre, where later he studied drawing, showing a great talent for caricature. Under the guidance of Boudin, his first real teacher, whom he met in 1858, he learned to prefer painting.

In 1859 he went to Paris and studied at the Swiss Academy, where he met Pissarro. More important for his future artistic development, however, were the discussions at the Brasserie des Martyrs and his acquaintance with the works of Delacroix.

After two years of military service in Algeria he returned in 1862 to Le Havre, where he spent the summer painting with Boudin and Jongkind. On his return to Paris he enrolled at Gleyre's studio, where he, Renoir, Bazille, and Sisley formed an independent group in revolt against the traditional teaching of their master.

Years of poverty and hardship followed. Monet worked in the forest of Fontainebleau, along the Seine and in Normandy. In 1866 his portrait of *Camille Doncieux* achieved a discrete success at the Salon.

In 1874 at the first Impressionist Show, of which he was one of the organizers, he exhibited his canvas *Impression—Sunrise,* which gave the group its name. These shows were repeated in 1876 and 1877, from 1879 through 1882, and in 1886. Monet

RENOIR *Portrait of Monet* (1875) Paris, Louvre

MONET *Two Fishermen,* Cambridge, Fogg Art Museum, Harvard University

did not participate in the fifth, sixth and eighth, because of controversy over selections by some of the promoters. He experienced great hardship, illness, poverty, loss of loved ones, scorn of critics and public. He finally achieved success and recognition and spent his last years painting at Giverny, where he died on December 5, 1926.

BERTHE MORISOT

Born at Bourges in 1841, of a bourgeois family, she began at eighteen, with her sister, to copy pictures in the Louvre.

Attracted by open-air painting, she became Corot's pupil in 1861 and painted with him at Ville-d'Avray.

Exhibited in the Salon from 1864 to 1868, the year in which she met Manet and agreed to pose for his painting *The Balcony.*

Her *View From the Gate at Lorient,* a work of delicate freshness admired by Manet, was exhibited at the Salon of 1870, but in 1876 she renounced the Salon, joined the Impressionist group and took part in their exhibit. The same year she married Manet's brother, Eugene, and a few years later had a daughter.

MORISOT *Self-Portrait* (1885-86) Mme. Ernest Rouart Collection

She was able to relate her work as a painter to her domestic life: children and domestic scenes indoors and out were her favorite subjects and

PISSARRO *Self-Portrait* (1903) London, Tate Gallery

PISSARRO *Rue Sainte-Vincent, Montmartre* (1860) New York, Private Collection

her pictures were exhibited at almost all the Impressionist shows. Renoir, Degas, Manet, and the writer Mallarmé often met at her home. She was left a widow in 1892 and died in Paris in 1895.

CAMILLE PISSARRO

Born at St. Thomas in the Antilles July 10, 1830. Was sent to Paris at an early age to receive a conventional education. Upon his return home he worked in his father's business and began to paint as a dilettante. In 1855, back in Paris, he became acquainted with Corot and studied first at the School of Fine Arts and then at the Swiss Academy, where he met Monet and Cézanne. Decisive for him in this period was his acquaintance with Courbet, who introduced him to the group of "realists" and led him away from Corot's influence.

In 1863 he took part in the Salon des Refusés and in 1865 and 1866 established firm friendship with the group of the Café Guerbois. In 1874 he was one of the participants in the first Impressionist show. He was the only one to show at all their exhibits, although for him, with six children to support, the difficulties against which all the Impressionists had to struggle were particularly hard.

The dealer Durand-Ruel organized a one-man show for him in 1883. In 1885 he came in contact with Seurat and Signac and with Pointilism and sided with the Divisionists in the show of 1886, but toward 1890 he abandoned the new researches and returned to "less scientific" painting.

In spite of a serious eye ailment he continued to work until his death, November 13, 1903.

PIERRE AUGUSTE RENOIR

Born in Limoges, February 25, 1841, to a family of artisans. When he was four his family moved to Paris, where his father, a humble tailor, hoped to better his precarious economic situation. At fourteen he entered a night school of drawing, working during the day as a porcelain decorator, and later as a decorator of fans and silks. He enrolled in the School of Fine Arts in 1862, at Gleyre's studio, where he met Monet, Sisley, and Bazille. In 1863 he went often to the Louvre to copy the old masters and to the forest of Fontainebleau, where he met Diaz, the former teacher of the Barbizon School, who taught him a love of nature and of color.

In 1868 his *Lise* was accepted by the Salon and achieved a moderate success. At this time Renoir frequented the group of the Café Guerbois: Monet, Degas, Pissarro, Cézanne, Fantin-Latour, the writer Zola, the photographer Nadar. With them he organized the first show of Impressionist works in 1874 in Nadar's studio. Because of disagreements with Degas he failed to exhibit in the shows of 1880 and 1886.

In 1881 he made a journey to Italy. His acquaintance with the work of Raphael and the frescoes of Pompeii influenced his later style.

Renoir began to enjoy a degree of reputation and economic well-being. He painted swiftly and continued to paint even when severe rheumatism forced him to have his brush strapped to his arm. He died at Cagnes, December 3, 1919, retaining to the last his enthusiasm and creative energy.

RENOIR *Heads of Women*, Paris, Robert Lebel Collection

RENOIR *Self-Portrait* (c. 1875) Formerly Dr. de Bellio Collection.

ALFRED SISLEY

Born in Paris, October 30, 1839, of English parents. At eighteen he was sent to London to prepare for a business career. But he had already shown an interest in art and in 1862, on his return to Paris, he obtained his family's permission to dedicate himself completely to painting. He enrolled at the School of Fine Arts, at Gleyre's studio, where he became friendly with Monet and Renoir. Induced by Monet, he began to paint out of doors. When Gleyre closed his studio Sisley painted at Fontainebleau, in Normandy and in the environs of Paris, in close collaboration with his friends, Monet, Renoir, and Pissarro. His paintings were accepted by the Salons of 1866, 1868, 1870 and refused by that of 1869.

Because of a financial upset caused by the war in 1870, Sisley was forced from then on to struggle against economic difficulties.

In 1874 he took part in the first Impressionist show. He also participated in the second (1876), third (1877), and seventh (1882). In 1883 Durand-Ruel organized the first one-man show of his works.

From 1890 Sisley showed at the annual exposition of the semiofficial National Society, but without great success.

He died in 1899 at Moret on the Loing, without ever having enjoyed real success.

RENOIR *Alfred Sisley and His Wife* (1868) Cologne, Wallraf Richartz Museum

SISLEY *Church at Moret,* Budapest, Museum of Fine Arts

JAMES McNEILL WHISTLER

Born in Lowell, Massachusetts, in 1834, he moved in 1843 with his family to Russia. After his father's death in 1849 he returned to America. In 1851 he entered the Military Academy at West Point, but, intolerant of discipline, he was expelled in 1854. The following year he went to Europe, determined to devote himself to painting. At Paris he attended Gleyre's courses at the Academy and visited the Realist Show of Courbet, which profoundly influenced his painting. Courbet himself was struck by a picture of Whistler's at the studio of Bonvin in 1859, and from that time Whistler was able to go, with his friend Fantin-Latour, to Courbet for advice. He moved to London in 1859 and through his friends Rossetti and Swinburne came in contact with the Pre-Raphaelite movement. In 1863 he exhibited at the Salon des Refusés and in 1865 painted at Trouville with Courbet. But he decided to abandon Courbet's type of naturalism and look for other means of artistic expression. In the years after 1870 he made the portraits that he called "Arrangements" and the "Nocturnes." In 1877 he brought suit against Ruskin for slander, and in 1885 defended his art at the famous meeting called the "Ten O'clock Lecture." He died in London in 1903.

WHISTLER *Self-Pertrait* (c. 1890) Washington, D.C., Freer Gallery of Art

WHISTLER *Studies of Loïe Fuller Dancing* (1895) Glasgow, University Art Collection

List of Illustrations

51 Pierre Auguste Renoir *The First Outing (La Première Sortie),* 1876, London, Tate Gallery
52 Pierre Auguste Renoir *The Loge,* 1874, London, Courtauld Institute
53 Pierre Auguste Renoir *Portrait of Madame Henriot,* 1877, Washington, D.C., National Gallery of Art (Gift of Adele R. Levy Fund Inc.)
54 Edgar Degas *Café Concert at les Ambassadeurs* (detail) 1876-77, Lyons, Musée des Beaux-Arts
55 Claude Monet *Rue Montargueil with Flags,* 1878, Rouen, Musée des Beaux-Arts
56 Alfred Sisley *Flood at Pont-Marly,* 1876, Paris, Louvre
57 Camille Pissarro *The Hermitage at Pontoise,* 1878, Basel, Kunstmuseum
58 Edgar Degas *The Rehearsal,* 1877, Glasgow Art Gallery and Museum, Sir William Burrell Collection
59 Edgar Degas *Rehearsal on the Stage,* 1878-79, New York, Metropolitan Museum of Art, Havemeyer Collection
60 Berthe Morisot *Young Woman Sewing in a Garden,* 1881, Pau, Musée des Beaux-Arts
61 Berthe Morisot *The Little Girl from Nice,* c. 1888-89, Lyons, Musée des Beaux-Arts
62 Mary Cassatt *The Sisters,* c. 1885, Glasgow Art Gallery and Museum, Sir William Burrell Collection
63 Berthe Morisot *The Butterfly Chase,* 1874, Paris, Louvre
64 Gustave Caillebotte *Paris in the Snow,* 1886, Geneva, Modern Art Fund
65 J. B. Armand Guillaumin *Outskirts of Paris,* 1873, Montpellier, Musée des Beaux-Arts
66 Edouard Manet *A Bar at the Folies-Bergère,* 1881-82, London, Courtauld Institute
67 Edouard Manet *The Model for the Folies-Bergère Bar* (detail) 1881, Dijon, Musée des Beaux-Arts
68 Alfred Sisley *The Tugboat,* c. 1883, Paris, Musée du Petit Palais
69 Camille Pissarro *The Wheelbarrow,* c. 1881, Paris, Louvre
70 Claude Monet *Poplars on the River Epte,* 1890, London, Tate Gallery
71 Claude Monet *Rouen Cathedral: The Façade in Sunlight,* 1894, Paris, Louvre
72 Pierre Auguste Renoir *Vase of Chrysanthemums,* Rouen, Musée des Beaux-Arts
73 Pierre Auguste Renoir *Blond Bather,* 1881, Turin, Private Collection
74 Alfred Sisley *The Banks of the Seine: Wind Blowing,* 1894, Rouen, Musée des Beaux-Arts
75 Camille Pissarro *The First February Rays at Bazincourt,* 1893, Otterlo, Rijksmuseum Kröller-Müller
76 Claude Monet *Waterlilies* (detail) c. 1910, Zurich, Kunsthaus
77 Camille Pissarro *The Louvre, Morning, Snow Effect,* 1902, London, Tate Gallery
78 Edgar Degas *After the Bath: Woman Drying Her Feet,* c. 1886, Paris, Louvre